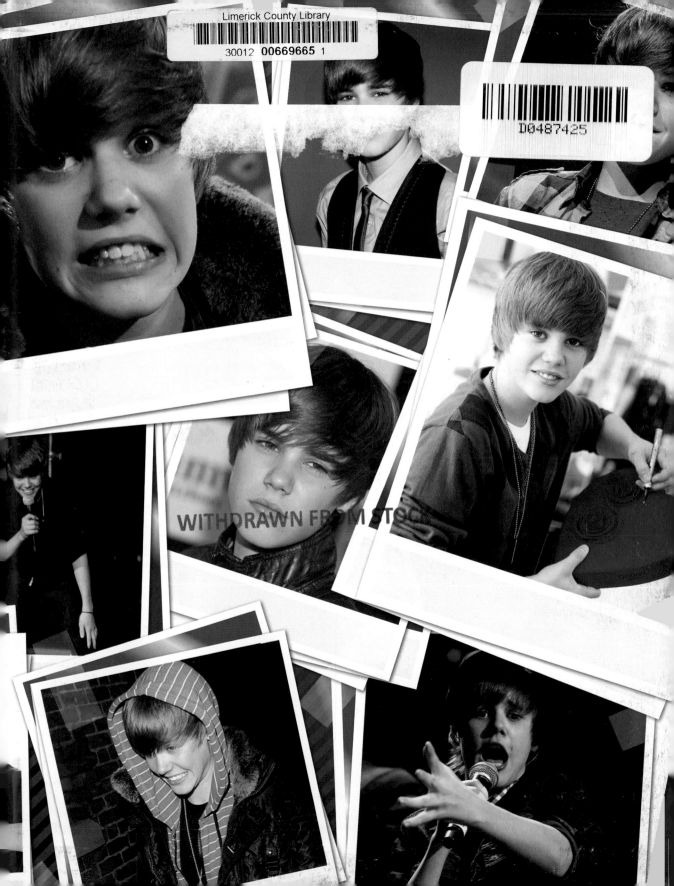

100% JUSTIN BIEBER: THE UNOFFICIAL BIOGRAPHY

A BANTAM BOOK 978 0 553 82271 7

First published in Great Britain by Bantam, an imprint of Random House Children's Books
A Random House Group Company

Bantam edition published 2010
1 3 5 7 9 10 8 6 4 2
Text copyright © Bantam Books, 2010

Design by Shubrook Bros. Creative
www.shubrookbros.com

Bantam Books are published by Random House Children's Books,
61-63 Uxbridge Road, London W5 5SA

www.rbooks.co.uk
www.kidsatrandomhouse.co.uk

Addresses for companies within The Random House Group Limited can be found at:
www.randomhouse.co.uk/offices.htm

THE RANDOM HOUSE GROUP Limited Reg. No. 954009

A CIP catalogue record for this book is available from the British Library

Printed and bound in Italy

EVIE PARKER

100% JUSTIN BIEBER

THE UNOFFICIAL BIOGRAPHY

BANTAM
BOOKS

CONTENTS

Page
32
Justin's Photo
Gallery

Page
22
Love Is in
the Air ...

THE MUSIC

He may just be 16 years old, but Justin appreciates all kinds of music!

A GOOD INFLUENCE...

Describing his own sound as 'pop R&B', Justin grew up listening to Michael Jackson, Stevie Wonder and Boyz II Men. But whilst some of this music is older than he is, he's still one of the most contemporary artists around.

"I had people I looked up to, but I would never try to be like anybody. I've learnt a lot from listening to Michael Jackson and Boyz II Men though."

"I think people can appreciate my music because I really show my heart when I sing. I think I can grow as an artist and my fans will grow with me."

JB's favourite albums of all time:

- Exclusive, Chris Brown
- Graduation, Kanye West
- Fully Completely, The Tragically Hip
- Confessions (natch!), Usher
- Because of You, Ne-Yo
- Appetite for Destruction, Guns N' Roses
- Evolution, Boyz II Men
- Thriller, Michael Jackson
- Bad, Michael Jackson
- II, Boyz II Men

USHER

In the blue corner we have. . . Usher!

"Usher on JB: His voice was magical and his personality was so keen"

Birth name:	Usher Raymond IV
Born:	October 14, 1978 Dallas, Texas, United States
Origin:	Chattanooga, Tennessee, United States Atlanta, Georgia, United States
Genres:	R&B, soul, pop
Occupations:	Singer-songwriter, music executive, actor, record producer
Years active:	1990–present
Labels:	LaFace, Arista
Associated acts:	NuBeginnings
Website:	www.usherworld...

Usher regretted not signing for him when [he] met in the car park of [...] By the time [...] -Beebs' singing online [...] Braun a call, Justin [...] there first. JT was [...] the online star to his [...] act quickly!

After meeting JB sing, JT, Scooter

A KOUT!

Usher Bieber's

"Sometimes he's like a little brother or a son to me." Usher

100% JUSTIN BIEBER
THE UNOFFICIAL BIOGRAPHY

NICOLE SCHERZINGER
Beebs reckons she's GORGEOUS!

Romantic evening he has to have:

If I wa[s] cooking for a g[irl] probabl[y] her a[nd] di[nner]

tin's dream has to have:
Nice eyes
Nice smile
Great sense of humour

Demi Lovato

n Fox

Justin Bieber
HIS WORLD

He's hotter than the Jonas Brothers; all three of them put together! With an amazing voice, super-cute smile and sparkling personality, Justin Bieber is the awesome new pop sensation that's taking the planet by storm! If you've caught a bad dose of Bieber fever, then read on!

Name:	Justin Drew Bieber
Birthday:	March 1, 1994
Star sign:	Pisces
Height:	5ft 3in
Home town:	Stratford, Ontario, Canada
Brothers and sisters:	He has a younger sister and step-brother
Nicknames:	J-Beebs, Beebs, JB
Pets:	A dog called Sam. He's a papillon.
Bad habits:	Eating too much candy!

In five years' time...

"I hope to have won a Grammy and done some acting. I'd love to be in a film."

When he's not in the recording studio...

"I'm just a regular kid. I like to hang out with my friends, play sport, go to the movies, go bowling, stuff like that."

Music maestro ...

J-Beebs taught himself to play the piano, drums, guitar and trumpet.

If he wasn't a singer ...

👀 I'd be playing hockey in the NHL. 👀

FROM BUSKER TO

See how Justin Bieber's made his meteoric rise to super-stardom!

IN THE BEGINNING...

Justin grew up in a really musical family. His dad played the guitar and his mum sang. Although his parents split up when he was really young, it didn't stop Justin pursuing his love of music. He started playing the drums when he was just two years old and by the age of twelve he had taught himself to play the drums, guitar, piano and trumpet.

At school, Justin was a pretty normal kid. He loved sport (especially football and ice hockey) and in his spare time he used to play the guitar, busking around Stratford.

DID YOU KNOW?

Bieber is the first artist to have all songs from a single album to chart in the U.S. Hot 100.

Justin's most watched cover songs

1 "With You", Chris Brown
2 "Cry Me a River", Justin Timberlake
3 "Wait for You", Elliot Yamin
4 "Fallin'", Alicia Keys
5 "You and Me", Lifehouse

HEADLINER

2ND PLACE ISN'T THAT BAD...

In 2007, at the age of twelve, Justin entered a local singing competition in his hometown; he came second. His mum, Pattie, posted the video of him singing on YouTube so that friends and family who hadn't been able to make the concert could see his performance. But rather than just his family watching the post, hundreds and thousands of people were checking out Justin's singing. His mum added more and more posts, and pretty soon Justin had caught the attention of a seriously cool hip-hop producer in Atlanta, Georgia. And that's when things really started to get crazy!

DID YOU KNOW?

JB has had millions of online hits since he uploaded his videos!

A DIAMOND IN THE ROUGH ...

Scooter Braun was surfing the internet, searching for new talent, when he came across Justin's posts on You-Tube. According to Braun, it was when he saw a clip of Justin busking that he knew he'd found the raw talent he was looking for. Scooter was a massive Michael Jackson fan and wanted to find someone who could perform and sing the kind of songs that Michael had done when he was a kid. He was so impressed that he set out to find him.

DID YOU KNOW?
The first album Justin owned featured songs by Barney!

Justin with his mum, Pattie.

THE SEARCH IS ON...

Scooter managed to track Justin down by calling three school boards in the area. He asked if they knew Justin and if so, could they ask his mum to give him a call. When Justin's mum, Pattie, first heard the news she was pretty wary, but after having a long chat with Scooter on the phone, she was convinced that this might be a great opportunity for Justin. Braun flew both Justin and Pattie down to Atlanta straight away. It was the first time Justin had ever been on a plane, but it certainly wasn't going to be the last!

A CHANCE ENCOUNTER...

In a studio car park, Justin bumped into Usher. He was a massive fan and ran up to the star to ask if he could sing for him. A little fazed, Usher politely declined, but just weeks later when Usher had seen Justin's clips on the internet, Braun got a call from the hip-hop star asking to meet with him to discuss the possibility of signing him to his record label. Unfortunately for Usher, Justin had a similar meeting already set up with another record label, one owned by Justin Timberlake...

DID YOU KNOW?
Justin Bieber can apparently fix a Rubix cube in less than 2 minutes!

The fight to sign Justin Bieber was on! It was Usher in the blue corner, and Justin Timberlake in the red, but who would be crowned the Bieber champ?

JUSTIN TIMBERLAKE

In the red corner we have... Justin Timberlake!

Birth name:	Justin Randall Timberlake
Born:	January 31, 1981 Memphis, Tennessee, United States
Lives:	Shelby Forest, Tennessee, United States
Genres:	R&B, dance, electronic, pop
Occupations:	Singer-songwriter, musician, record producer, dancer, actor
Instruments:	Vocals, keyboards, guitar, beatboxing
Years active:	1993-present
Labels:	Jive
Associated acts:	'N Sync, The 9's

ROUND 1

When Justin's mum, Pattie, posted home-made videos of her son singing online, she didn't expect it to start a bidding war with two of the biggest music stars in the world!

So it must have been a pretty nice surprise when she got a call to schedule a meeting for her and JB with none other than megastar Justin Timberlake!

Timberlake wanted to sign JB to his own label, Tenman Records. His first find for the label was another YouTube phenomenon, 21-year-old Esmée Denters, and when Timberlake heard JB sing "Cry Me a River" online, he knew straight away that he wanted to sign Bieber up too.

USHER

In the blue corner we have ... Usher!

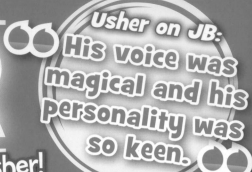

Usher on JB:
His voice was magical and his personality was so keen.

ROUND 2

Birth name:	Usher Raymond IV
Born:	October 14, 1978 Dallas, Texas, United States
Lives:	Chattanooga, Tennessee, United States Atlanta, Georgia, United States
Genres:	R&B, soul, pop
Occupations:	Singer-songwriter, music executive, actor, record producer
Years active:	1990-present
Labels:	LaFace, Arista
Associated acts:	NuBeginnings

We reckon Usher regretted not letting JB sing for him when they first met in the car park of the recording studio! By the time Usher had checked out J-Beebs' singing online and given Scooter Braun a call, Justin Timberlake had got there first. JT was interested in signing the online star to his label; Usher needed to act quickly!

After meeting again with both Usher and JT, Scooter Braun finally arranged a deal with ... Usher! Having shot to fame at an early age himself, superstar Usher would be the perfect mentor to JB. One of the biggest pieces of advice he has given the young star so far is to "stay humble and stay on the right path, then anything's possible".

IT'S A KNOCKOUT!

Usher wins the title of Justin Bieber's co-producer!

> **Sometimes he's like a little brother or a son to me.**
> Usher

THE MUSIC

He's only sixteen years old, but Justin appreciates all kinds of music!

A GOOD INFLUENCE...

Describing his own sound as "pop R&B", Justin grew up listening to Michael Jackson, Stevie Wonder and Boyz II Men. But whilst some of this music is older than he is, he's still one of the most contemporary artists around.

"I had people I looked up to, but I would never try to be like anybody. I've learnt a lot from listening to Michael Jackson and Boyz II Men though."

JB

JB's favourite albums of all time!

10 *Exclusive*, Chris Brown
9 *Graduation*, Kanye West
8 *Fully Completely*, The Tragically Hip
7 *Confessions* (natch!), Usher
6 *Because of You*, Ne-Yo
5 *Appetite for Destruction*, Guns N' Roses
4 *Evolution*, Boyz II Men
3 *Thriller*, Michael Jackson
2 *Bad*, Michael Jackson
1 *II*, Boyz II Men

> "I think people can appreciate my music because I really show my heart when I sing. I think I can grow as an artist and my fans will grow with me."
>
> JB

DREAM TEAM ...

He's already worked with some of the best producers and writers in the business, including Tricky Stewart and The-Dream, the team who produced Rihanna's "Umbrella" and Beyoncé's "Single Ladies". "Making the album was just a blast, " says JB, "and I think that having so much fun was reflected in it. I worked with some really great people."

So who would JB like to collaborate with next? Beyoncé of course!

19

WORD UP!

Take a peek at the wordsearch below and see if you can spot all the Bieber-related words hidden inside it.

TAYLOR SWIFT   ATLANTA
USHER   CANADA
TIMBERLAKE   BLUE
MY WORLD   BEYONCE
FOOT   PETA

```
T G A X P R E H S U L
A I F E E Q T C A N S
Y B M H I U O A T R N
L A D B E Y O N C E X
O Y K L E R K A I G Q
R P E U S R T D O B U
S A X E A T L A N T A
W F D A R G I A M E T
I E K I P A D C K I E
F O O T X Y Z E R E P
T V H E A R G I S T N
Z P O D L R O W Y M X
```

SPOT THE BIEBER BOO-BOOS!

Take a close look at these two pictures of Justin Bieber and see if you can spot all ten differences between them.

21

LOVE IS IN THE AIR...

Phew! It's getting hot in here! If you've got a bad dose of Bieber fever then check out what makes J-Beebs tick when it comes to all things luuuuuurve and romance!

HOT QUESTION?

Was J-Beebs' hit single, "One Time", about a specific girl?

"There's not a specific girl, it goes out to all you girls!" – Swoon!

LOVE STATS

First kiss:	Age 13.
Last date:	Justin hasn't had a chance to go on a date in about three years.
Celeb or pleb:	It doesn't matter whether a girl's famous or not. JB has said he'd go out with any girl if he fell in love with her. Ahhhh!
In his own words:	"I'm single and ready to mingle!" – Girls, look out!

BIEBER'S BEAUTIES...

Check out the famous hotties that J-Beebs has got a crush on!

RIHANNA
She gave J-Beebs a cheeky peck on the cheek!

BEYONCÉ
She's Bieber's no.1 lady. Jay-Z had better watch out!

FOREVER FRIENDS

He's the boy all the girls want to date. But what do JB's friends think about him and his newfound fame?

P. Diddy to Justin:

" As soon as you turn 16, I'm gonna give you my Lamborghini. The keys are yours. "

Keri Hilson on Justin:

" His effect on kids is like, what? He goes on stage after me and all he has to do is make this heart with his hands and those kids scream shriekingly loud. "

THE OLDIES...

Justin has loads of celeb pals, but that doesn't mean he's forgotten his old friends from back home. His BFFs are his childhood friends Chaz Somers and Ryan Butler (who you might recognize from his video "One Time"). JB thanks them both in the liner notes to his seven-song EP for "helping me stay Justin". They've been friends since they were six years old!

Justin is such a good friend, that he makes sure he sees Chaz and Ryan at least once a month and he flies them out to see him whenever he can. Ahhh...

THE NEW BF...

Now living in Atlanta, he's had to make some new friends, and he's found a great friend in Atlanta native, Christian Beadles. Christian posts loads of YouTube videos, many with him and Bieber just messing around and having fun. JB once dated Christian's older sister, Caitlin, but they broke up.

Usher on Justin:
Justin is such an incredibly talented young man. He sang my own song to me and he actually sang it a bit better than me!

I think it's really important to have your close friends around you.

Rihanna on Justin:
He's a cutie-pie!

Justin's teacher:
He has no fear. I couldn't believe how quickly he could pick things up – whether it was soccer, basketball, singing or dancing.

Justin on Taylor Swift:
She's amazing and a really nice girl. We're friends. She's the sweetest girl and she says I've got a good head on my shoulders.

THE CELEBS...

Bieber is lapping up the attention as he rides the wave of pop music celebrity. Now that he's working alongside lots of stars, they can't help but love the Beebs too!

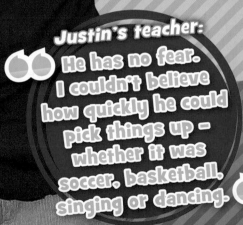

25

CRAZY TIMES

Justin hasn't been in the public eye for that long, but he's already had his fair share of mad moments!

BIEBER FEVER...

The craziest moment must have been when JB nearly got arrested in a mall in Long Island! He was supposed to perform there to promote his album, but it had to be cancelled because over 3,000 screaming fans got totally out of control and the police had to be called.

Trying to get things under control, Justin tweeted to his fans:

 Justin Bieber

The event at Roosevelt Mall is cancelled. Please go home. The police have already arrested one person from my camp. I don't want anyone hurt.
12:04 PM

They are not allowing me to come into the mall. If you don't leave, I and my fans will be arrested as the police just told us.
12:32 PM

I'm sorry to everyone who was in Long Island at the Mall 2day. I was just trying to come meet fans and never meant to disappoint anyone.
1:08 PM

CRINGE!

JB says his most embarrassing moment was when he broke his foot on stage whilst performing with Taylor Swift. He said, "I was opening up for Taylor which was a lot of fun – although it definitely wasn't fun when I broke my foot. I was running and there was a little dip in the stage and I rolled my ankle and broke it!" Ouchie!

CRINGE!

It's pretty clear by now that JB has a HUGE crush on Beyoncé. But just in case a few people didn't know, he announced it loud and clear at the 52nd Annual Grammys! When presenting an award, Bieber accidentally said Beyoncé's name instead of Bon Jovi... but was it truly an accident?

"Maybe I was trying to get Beyoncé's attention," he joked. Well, it certainly worked! Jay-Z had better watch out!

BIEBER-MANIA!

Justin has always been really grateful for all the love and support he gets from his fans, so we thought he'd like it if we dedicated a whole page to you guys!

Top 5 crazy fan moments

1 One fan's mum was willing to get a tattoo of a radio DJ done on her back just so she could get Justin Bieber concert tickets for her daughter. Ouch!

2 Whilst in New York he only managed to walk two blocks by himself before he got mobbed by screaming fans!

3 In Seattle, one fan went to give JB a hug but got so carried away she ended up tackling him and pulled the poor guy to the ground!

4 He was doing a radio interview when he mentioned to a fan that he was really hungry. The lovely girl went and bought him a Big Mac, but unfortunately for J-Beebs, his mum wouldn't let him eat it!

5 When he held a small concert in New York, girls started queuing for tickets at 8:45 in the morning; the gig wasn't due to start till 6pm! Now *that's* dedication.

Weirdest crowd-sign he's ever read?
BRING THE COUGARS ON STAGE

If you're in the crowd at a Justin Bieber concert, how can you get yourself noticed?

● **SMILE!** Justin is massively appreciative of all his fans. He's said that nothing makes him happier than watching a crowd of smiling people because then he knows he's doing something they like and that they want to be there for.

● **SCREAM!** Justin reckons that screaming the loudest will make you stand out from the crowd.

● **GO WILD!** When he's on stage he gets a massive buzz from everybody's energy. It makes him feel really good and is part of the reason he puts on such a great show.

Would he ever date a fan?
Not yet, but yet is the key word.
– There's hope for us all!

PICTURE PERFECT

100% JUSTIN BIEBER

THE UNOFFICIAL BIOGRAPHY

JB IN OUR WORDS

Ever wonder what JB thinks about?
We do. *All* the time!

No one touches the J-Bob
but J-Beebs!

We wish Justin would sing
to us like that!

You can't hide
from us, JB!

Look out John Mayer, there's
a JB on your shoulder!

J-Beebs does a great
Bugs Bunny impression!

Uh-oh! Has Bieber made a boo-boo?

"I said *four* Big Macs!"

Go on, hit that high note, JB.
You can do it!

"Sam did *what* in my trailer?"

33

10 REASONS WHY WE LOVE JUSTIN

Ok, apart from the great voice, cute face, amazing hair and sparkling personality, here are ten more reasons to love Justin Bieber...

1 Justin thinks girls look better without make-up!

2 He used to busk outside the Avon Theatre in his home town. He saved all the money he made and took his mum and sister on the family's first ever holiday to Disneyland, Florida.

3 He's a spokesman for PETA (People for the Ethical Treatment of Animals).

4 His pet dog, Sam, came from an animal shelter.

5 He thinks British girls are cute and have cute accents.

6 His mum is his favourite person in the whole world.

7 When he broke his foot on stage with Taylor Swift, he finished the song and still managed to perform the next night! What a trooper.

8 He's totally humble. After singing to help raise money for the Haitian earthquake he posted on Twitter: "Tonight was one of the greatest experiences of my life... I'm a small-town kid who started a YouTube page for fun three years ago. Tonight I sang with some of my heroes. Still in shock and super grateful."

9 If he had a million dollars, the first thing he'd buy would be a house for his mum!

10 He's so talented that he taught himself how to play the drums, piano, guitar and trumpet!

DID YOU KNOW?
JB once signed 50 posters in under three minutes.

DO YOU HAVE T[H

Find out if you have what it takes to be the next hot pop sensation!

Your fave song comes on the radio. Do you...
A. Sing along at the top of your voice?
B. Hum along quietly?

A

Your hairbrush is...
A. Your microphone.
B. What you use to brush your hair.

A

B

B

In the school talent show you...
A. Perform an awesome number.
B. Help out backstage with the sound and lighting.

A

Your friend is taking a photo: do you...
A. Fix your hair and take prime spot in front of the camera?
B. Head for the back and hide?

A

B

B

A

Your friends would describe you as...
A. Bubbly and outgoing.
B. Sweet and shy.

B

When you go to a party do you...
A. Dress up to the max!
B. Throw on a pair of jeans and a pretty top.

36

You hear cheering: do you...
A. Take a bow – it must be for you!
B. Go and find out what's going on?

Your dream birthday party would be...
A. Riding in a limo with JB blasting on the stereo.
B. A picnic in the park with your best mates.

Super Star!
You've got the confidence and charisma that'll take you to the top! So get set to work hard and get ready to take the world by storm!

Karaoke is...
A. 100% AWESOME!
B. Great fun! But only when you sing in a group.

You'd never leave the house without...
A. Your iPod!
B. Your diary.

Shining Star!
You love a good sing along, but you're happy not to be lead! Your friends love that about you, which is why you're so popular!

Complete this sentence. Fame and fortune is...
A. All I ever dream about.
B. OK, but I'm happy without it.

Which would you pick?
A. Limelight.
B. Candlelight.

When you're in class are you usually...
A. The centre of attention?
B. Hiding behind a pile of books?

Silent Star!
Although you're not openly seeking super-stardom, your quiet self-confidence and sense of style mean you definitely don't lack in star quality!

JB'S FAVOURITE THINGS

We know why we love JB! But do you know what he loves? Here's where we quiz J-Beebs on a few of his favourite things...

GENERAL STUFF

Favourite colour: blue
Favourite animal: dog
Favourite number: six
Favourite slang word: "shawty"
Favourite British words: "brilliant", "geezer"
Favourite sport: football and ice hockey
Favourite video game: NBA 2K9
Favourite place in the world: I've been to a lot of places around the world but my favourite place is still my hometown.
Favourite moment: When my baby sister was born.

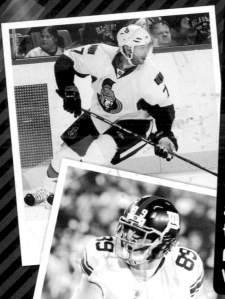

FOOD AND DRINK

Favourite food: spaghetti
Favourite dessert: apple pie
Favourite drink: orange juice
Favourite cereal: Captain Crunch

MUSIC

Favourite singer: Michael Jackson
Favourite album: II, Boyz II Men
Favourite karaoke song: "Appetite for Destruction", Guns N' Roses

DID YOU KNOW?

JB has said he doesn't dream. Apparently he just falls asleep, sees black, and then wakes up.

MOVIES AND TV

Favourite TV show: Smallville
Favourite film: Rocky
Favourite chic flick: The Notebook

JB IN COLOUR

Grab your pens and bring J-Beebs to life!

CROSSWORD

Get in the Bieberzone and complete this crossword if you can!

ACROSS

1) In "One Less Lonely Girl", what does JB's love interest drop?
4) What is Justin's nationality?
8) Justin is good at this sport.
9) What is the name of Justin's best friend?
10) Justin likes a girl who has a lovely _____.

DOWN

2) Where did Justin move to when he got signed?
3) What does Justin use to get his trademark hairstyle?
5) Justin received a kiss from this female singer.
6) What piece of clothing does Justin often wear?
7) Justin has sung for this President.

SAY WHAT?

We think Justin comes out with some awesome one-liners, and here's a few of his best ones!

If I could do anything I'd probably go to space with Chuck Norris.

Now, that sounds like fun!

The harder you work, the more successful you can be. This is just the beginning for me.

We can't wait to see more of you!

I could take anyone. I'm a kung-fu ninja! I have a double black belt.

About Usher:

He's just a regular cat like you and me.

What? Only like the coolest cat on the block!

" I like to goof off and be the centre of attention. "

And that's just where we like you to be, Justin!

" If I wasn't a pop star I'd be a chef. I would cook all the lovely ladies a nice dinner "

We'd eat at your restaurant anytime!

On who'd win in a fight between him and the Jonas Brothers:

" I think I could take all three! I'm a beast! "

Go, Justin!

43

STAR STYLE

No matter what he's doing, J-Beebs always looks great! Whether he's glamming it up at an awards ceremony or just hanging out with his friends, JB is a tween fashion icon!

SWAGGERIFIC...

Usher hooked JB up with his very own swagger coach to help him with his confidence and style. JB calls it "staying swaggerific". We may not all be this lucky, but Justin shows us that being comfortable in what you wear is the most important style lesson around.

Justin's favourite shop:
AMERICAN APPAREL

Favourite item of clothing
66 **I like to wear my hat a lot of times.** 99

DID YOU KNOW?
JB has invisible braces!

THE J-BOB!

We can't have a style section without commenting on JB's trademark hair! When asked how he gets that glossy, forward-sitting look, he says, "After I shower, I blow dry my hair and just shake it and it goes like that." But whilst it may seem low-maintenance, that doesn't mean he likes it being ruffled up by people! "Yeah, that can be annoying." Uh-oh, hands off!

Cap

Chain

T-shirt

STEAL HIS STYLE!

JB dresses simply and keeps his outfits youthful and casual. He rocks a number of looks, but his main style staples are:

Checked shirt

Hoodie

Long-sleeved T-shirt

FACE OFF!

These music stars have all been a big influence on Justin. Can you work out who's who?

1..	4..
2..	5..
3..	

ALL MIXED UP!

Can you unscramble these words to find the right answers?

1 He is signed to Nialds Efd Mja records.

2 If Justin wasn't a singer, he'd like to be a Efch.

3 "Anm ni eth Rrmroi" is Justin's fave Michael Jackson song.

4 Justin has been in the US show *Ture Jksoacn PV*.

5 Justin's favourite Beyoncé video is "Lgesin Asdeil".

6 Saludcri guest stars in one of Justin's singles.

1...
2...
3...
4...
5...
6...

IT'S PARTY TIME!

So you and all your mates are massive Bieber fans, what's the most fun thing to do to show your appreciation of all things J-Beebs? Throw a Bieber party, of course!

OH, CANADA!

So, Canada's a pretty cool country, J-Beebs has said that his favourite place in the world is still his home town. But apart from the awesome Justin Bieber, what other cool stuff is Canada famous for?

MOUNTIES

They're bold, they're brave and they wear red so well!

Have a blue-clothes dress code! That's JB's fave colour. Don't forget your hairbrush for sing-a-long party fun! Line up some tunes from Usher, Michael Jackson, Taylor Swift and Boys II Men to help get into the Bieber vibe.

MAPLE SYRUP

Where would pancakes be without maple syrup?

Go all out to celebrate everything Canadian by making some fun bunting using the country's flag.

Put the Grammy Awards on TV to celebrate Justin's awesome presenting skills.

Crank up J-Beebs' album My World on the stereo.

Pancakes with Canadian maple syrup make great party food.

NIAGARA FALLS

One of the most amazing places in the whole world.

Get ready to bust some amazing J-Beebs dance moves with your mates!

49

JB'S GUIDE TO BEC

Have you been bitten by the popstar bug? Do you dream of people screaming your name? Have you watched homemade videos of wannabe singers on YouTube, thinking, "I could do that!"? If so, our online singing sensation has words of advice on how to succeed.

Relax
" I like to play videogames just moments before going on stage. "

Be humble
" I think that being humble and being able to have the ability to show others a positive message and influence them in a positive way is the most important thing. "

Stay strong
" There are so many kid stars that have fallen down the wrong path because this is such a hard business and they lose themselves. "

" If you love to sing, be confident and post videos online. "

Have fun
Justin likes to take a day out of every week to just do his own thing – sometimes he'll just lie in bed all day. He also likes to hang out with friends, go to movies and just chill when he's not working.

Stay grounded
" It's very good to surround yourself with people who aren't just going to make you feel like you're bigger. I have my family to keep me grounded and I have really great people around me. "

His personal motto: Family first

ONLINE FAME

Justin's not the only one to find fame on the net!
Here are some other people who managed it too!

Lily Allen - she created a profile on myspace and made some of her recordings public before she was signed by her record label.

Savannah Outen - an American singer who has already appeared in countless tween magazines, Radio Disney Jams 11 album, and the new Tinkerbell Soundtrack.

Esmee Denters - Justin Timberlake signed this YouTube sensation to his label Tenman records after he saw her videos online.

PICTURE THIS!

100% JUSTIN BIEBER

THE UNOFFICIAL BIOGRAPHY

JUSTIN TRIVIA

How much do you know about everyone's favourite pint-sized pop star? Take this quiz to find out...

1

What is Justin's middle name?
- [ ] a. Nick
- [ ] b. Dan
- [ ] c. Drew

2

What star sign is Justin?
- [ ] a. Pisces
- [ ] b. Leo
- [ ] c. Gemini

3

The first instrument Justin learnt to play was...
- [ ] a. The piano
- [ ] b. The drums
- [ ] c. The trumpet

4

Justin's dog is called...
- [ ] a. P. Diddy
- [ ] b. Chuck
- [ ] c. Sam

54

Who is Justin's celebrity crush?

 5

- ☐ a. Vanessa Hudgens
- ☐ b. Kylie Minogue
- ☐ c. Beyoncé

Justin's manager is...

 6

- ☐ a. Scooter Braun
- ☐ b. Justin Timberlake
- ☐ c. His mum

What phobia does Justin suffer from?

7

- ☐ a. Claustrophobia
  (fear of small spaces)
- ☐ b. Arachnophobia
  (fear of spiders)
- ☐ c. Tetraphobia
  (fear of the number four)

8

What year was Justin born?

- ☐ a. 1995
- ☐ b. 1994
- ☐ c. 1993

Justin's first album is called...

9

- ☐ a. One Day
- ☐ b. My World
- ☐ c. Your Time

What is Justin's favourite colour?

10

- ☐ a. Green
- ☐ b. Blue
- ☐ c. Red

JUSTIN-OGRAPHY

MY WORLD

#	TITLE	WRITER/S	PRODUCER/S
1	"One Time"	Tricky Stewart, The-Dream, James Bunton, Corron Cole, Thabiso Nkhereanye	C. Stewart, Kuk Harrell, J. Bunton, C. Cole
2	"Favourite Girl"	Antea Birchett, Anesha Birchet, Dernst Emile II, Delisha Thomas	D. Emile II
3	"Down to Earth"	Justin Bieber, Midi Mafia, Mason Levy, Carlos Battey, Steven Battey	Midi Mafia
4	"Bigger"	Justin Bieber, Midi Mafia, Dapo Torimiro, Lonny Breaux	Midi Mafia, Dapo Torimiro
5	"One Less Lonely Girl"	Ezekiel Lewis, Balewa Muhammad, Sean Hamilton, Hyuk Shin, Usher Raymond IV	E. Lewis, B. Muhammad, S. Hamilton, H. Shin
6	"First Dance" (featuring Usher)	Justin Bieber, Usher Raymond IV, Jesse "Corparal" Wilson, Ryan Lovette, Dwight Reynolds, Alexander Parhm, Jr.	Pretty Boi Fresh
7	"Love me"	Peter Svensson, Nina Persson	DJ Frank E
BONUS TRACKS			
8	"Common Denominator" (U.S., Canadian and Australian iTunes bonus track)	Justin Bieber, Lashaunda "Babygirl" Carr	L. Carr
9	"One Less Lonely Girl" (French Adaptation; Canadian release only)	Ezekiel Lewis, Balewa Muhammad, Sean Hamilton, Hyuk Shin, Usher Raymond IV; translation: Andrée Watters	E. Lewis, B. Muhammad, S. Hamilton, H. Shin

FILMOGRAPHY

YEAR	TITLE	ROLE	NOTES
2009	True Jackson, VP	Himself	Guest star
2010	Silent Library	Himself	Guest star
2010	School Gyrls	Unknown	

A-Z OF JUSTIN

A **Avon Theatre** - JB's old busking haunt

B **Beyoncé** - we wish we were Beyoncé!

C **Charity** - JB's a spokesperson for PETA

D **Dancing** - he's got the moves!

E **Elissa Sursara** - JB has a crush on this actress

F **Foot** - JB broke his foot at a Taylor Swift concert

G **Guitar** - JB's instrument of choice

H **Hat** - JB's favourite item of clothing

I **Island Def Jam Records** - his label

J **Justin Timberlake** - even he wanted a piece of J-Beebs!

K **King of Pop** - Michael Jackson is one of Justin's biggest influences

L **Ludacris** - he collaborated with JB on "Baby"

M ***My World*** - JB's first album

N **Nicknames** - J-Beebs, Beebs, JB; he's got loads!

O **"One Time"** - JB's first single

P **Pattie** - JB's mum!

Q **Quality** - this is one word that really sums up JB!

R **Ryan** - his BFF!

S **Sam** - his pet pooch

T **Taylor Swift** - his celeb chum

U **Usher** - JB's co-producer and mentor

V **Vacation** - JB's first ever family holiday was to Florida

W **Warm-up** - JB knows the importance of vocal warm-ups before a gig

X **Xylophone** - JB can probably play this too!

Y **YouTube** - where he was first spotted

Z **Zip code** - information we wish we knew so we could visit him!

ANSWERS

Page 20
WORD UP!

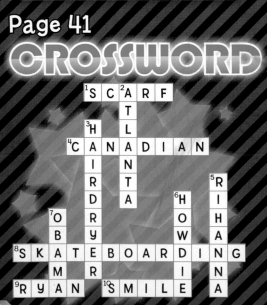

```
T G A X P R E H S U L
A I F E E Q T C A N S
y B M H I U O A T R N
L A D B E Y O N C E X
O y K L E R K A I G Q
R P E U S R T D O B U
S A X E A T L A N T A
W F D A R G I A M E T
I E K I P A D C K I E
F O O T X Y Z E R E P
T V H E A R G I S T N
Z P O D L R O W Y M X
```

Page 41
CROSSWORD

```
¹S C ²A R F
    T
  ³H T
⁴C A N A D I A N
  I N
  R T
  D A          ⁵R
  R    ⁶H       I
⁷O B  R    O   H
 M    Y    W   A
⁸S K A T E B O A R D I N G
 M    R    I   N
⁹R Y A N ¹⁰S M I L E  A
```

Page 21
SPOT THE BIEBER BOO-BOOS!

60